CRANKS

SOUPS & STARTERS

Compiled by Daphne Swann

To our customers worldwide

Cranks is indebted to the following people whose help in producing this book has been invaluable.

Jane Suthering, who devised, adapted and tested the recipes contained in this book and for her unfailing creativity, expertise and enthusiasm.

Jane Lydbury, illustrator.

Grant Symon, photographer.

Karen Boxell helped by Gail Moore, our two secretaries, for their patience, good humour and skills in the endless checking, collating and typing of this book.

© Text Cranks Ltd 1987
© The Work Guinness Superlatives Ltd 1987
© Illustrations Jane Lydbury 1987
© Photographs Grant Symon 1987

Published in Great Britain by Guinness Superlatives Ltd, 33 London Road, Enfield, Middlesex, England.

Designed by Newell and Sorrell, 14 Utopia Village, Chalcot Road, London NW1 8LH.

Cranks soups & starters
1. Soups   2. Cookery (Appetizers)
3. Cookery (Natural foods)
I. Cranks Limited
641.8'12   TX740

ISBN 0–85112–866–1

Printed in Italy by Arnoldo Mondadori Editore, Vicenza

INTRODUCTION

When Cranks opened its first restaurant 25 years ago (in Carnaby Street in London's Soho) its name exactly reflected how most people viewed wholefood and vegetarian restaurants – nutty in more senses than one! Now, of course, the lonely furrow that Cranks then ploughed has become the broad highway for a great many.

From the very beginning Cranks became something of a cult and throughout has remained the benchmark by which all other similar enterprizes have to be judged. Not only has there been an unswerving commitment to wholefood and vegetarian food without additives or preservatives (to this day Cranks still use flour from Pimhill Farm in Shropshire, which was one of the first to become totally organic) but there has also been a vigorous experimentation, innovation and creation of new dishes. And although now the food served at any of Cranks expanding family of restaurants is sophisticated by comparison with the relatively simple fare of the earliest days, there still remains a satisfying practicality and unfussiness in the recipes which is a refreshing change from the pretentiousness of many restaurants and cookbooks.

The continual creation of new dishes has, over the years, produced a vast number of tried and tested recipes – and it's from this repertoire of new dishes that the very best have been selected for inclusion in this series of books.

NOTES ON INGREDIENTS

Agar The vegetarian substitute for gelatine. It is derived from a sea vegetable and produces a slightly cloudy jelly when set. It is available as a powder or in flakes.

Apple concentrate This syrupy brown concentrated apple juice is available in bottles in most health food shops.

Arrowroot Used as a thickening agent, this white powder extracted from the rhizome of a herbaceous plant from the West Indies is believed to be helpful with digestive disorders.

Butter Cranks recommend using an unsalted butter. Vegetarian margarine may, of course, be substituted in all recipes where butter is stated.

Cheese Vegetable rennet is now used in some Cheddar and other hard cheese and these can be bought in all good health food shops. Curd cheese made from whole cow's milk, is a soft cheese usually set without rennet. Cottage cheese is a low fat curd cheese made from cooked skimmed cow's milk.

Chinese dried mushrooms Obtainable from Oriental shops, they are rather expensive but in our recipes only one or two are needed and their special flavour is important to the recipe.

Citrus fruits Thoroughly wash all citrus fruit rinds before using to remove any chemical deposits – better still – use organically grown fruit.

Coconut Can be bought in various forms – desiccated or shredded (which is finely grated and dried) or creamed. This is sold in bars or tubs and can be broken off and melted for use in cooking. Coconut milk powder is sold like dried milk. All can be found in good health food shops or oriental shops.

Eggs Cranks only use free range eggs in its bakeries and therefore recommend them in all the recipes. Many free range eggs are not graded but as a guideline we would use size 3. They are now readily available in most shops – do be sure to look for the label 'free range'.

Flour We use 100% wholemeal stoneground and organically grown flour in all our recipes – thus using the whole of the wheat berry. White flour has all the valuable bran and germ removed. *Soya* flour is a fine pale flour made from protein-rich soya beans.

Freezing Recipes which are suitable for freezing are marked by asterisks (∗∗∗).

Miso A salty brown paste made from fermented soya beans and a living food containing valuable enzymes which are destroyed by boiling.

Nutter An alternative to lard produced from nut oil and available from health food shops in blocks or tubs.

Oil Sunflower, safflower and soya oil are all good to use for cooking and salads being mild in flavour and low in saturated fats. However, olive oil gives a particularly good flavour to certain recipes.

Pot barley This is the wholegrain barley with only the outer husk removed. It will take longer to cook than the refined pearl barley.

Red kidney beans These must be fast boiled for a minimum of 15 minutes to destroy a poisonous substance they contain. They should never be sprouted for eating raw as they are toxic until thoroughly cooked.

Sea vegetables

Arame fine strands of dried seaweed available in sealed packs from health food shops.

Kombu is dried kelp sold in thick green strands. It makes a delicately flavoured stock.

Nori a seaweed sold in thin sheets which should be lightly toasted before using.

Soya sauce A dark salty sauce made from fermented soya beans.

Sugar Unrefined brown sugar is used in all Cranks recipes. It is free from artificial colouring and other additives and is available in five types: Demerara, light muscavado, muscavado, molasses and golden granulated. For authenticity check the country of origin, usually Mauritius.

Tahini A thick oily paste made from roasted sesame seeds rich in fats, protein and minerals. May be thinned down with water.

Tofu A soya bean curd with a soft delicate texture and pale in colour. Sold in slabs or slices, available plain, with herbs, smoked or marinated. It should be kept refrigerated. The softer consistency is called Silken Tofu.

Yoghourt Whole or skimmed milk is injected with a live bacteria and left to ferment to produce yoghourt. It is a good form of protein, low in fat if made with skimmed milk and a good source of calcium. Greek strained yoghourt is creamy and smoother than ordinary yoghourt and is an excellent substitute for cream.

WHOLE MEAL PASTRY CHART
easy guide to quantities

100% wholemeal flour	baking powder	½ butter ½ Nutter	water (approx)
4oz (100g)	1 tsp (5ml)	2oz (50 g)	4 tsp (20 ml)
5oz (150 g)	1½ tsp (7.5 ml)	2½oz (75g)	2 tbsp (30 ml)
6oz (175g)	1½ tsp (7.5 ml)	3oz (85 g)	2 tbsp (30 ml)
7oz (200 g)	2 tsp (10 ml)	3½ oz (100 g)	3 tbsp (45 ml)
9oz (250 g)	2½ tsp (12.5ml)	4½oz (125 g)	4 tbsp (60 ml)
10oz (300 g)	1 tbsp (15 ml)	5oz (150 g)	4 tbsp (60 ml)
12oz (350 g)	3 tbsp (15 ml)	6oz (175 g)	5 tbsp (75 ml)
14oz (400 g)	4 tbsp (20 ml)	7oz (200 g)	5 tbsp (75 ml)

Put the flour and baking powder into a basin. Rub in the fat until the mixture resembles fine crumbs. Add sufficient warm water to give a soft but manageable dough. Cover with cling film and leave at room temperature until ready to use.

US EQUIVALENTS

An American pint measures 16 fl oz (500 ml) and there are 2 cups (8 fl oz (250 ml) each) to the pint. The British pint is 20 fl oz (600 ml).

British Standard measuring spoons are:
1 teaspoon = 5 ml
1 tablespoon = 15 ml
Hence there are 3 teaspoons to one tablespoon.
An American tablespoon is 4 teaspoons (20 ml)

There is no easy guide for translating recipes from English to American but here are a few standard amounts.
1 cup butter = 8 oz (225 g)
1 cup sugar = 7 oz (200 g)
1 cup flour = 5 oz (150 g)

SOUPS & STARTERS

Some of Cranks popular favourites as well as a number of interesting new ideas appear in this book. The first section includes thick chunky soups like Courgette, Tomato & Walnut, served with hunks of wholemeal bread – a meal in itself – or delicately flavoured pureed soups such as Apricot and Orange or the more pungent Garlic Herb Soup and many other unusual ones like Curried Cream of Avocado.

Among the Starters are patés and dips, pastries and terrines, delicious salads like Stop-Go Salad – a profusion of red and green vegetables and fruits – or the piquant Iced Tomato Crush or Lemon & Avocado Sorbet for a really hot Summer's evening – there is a recipe for every occasion. Choose carefully to balance the starter with the rest of the meal.

BASIC VEGETABLE STOCK

These are the ideal vegetables for making up a good tasty stock – always keep some in the refrigerator at the ready! Other leaf or root vegetables may be substituted.

Water 2 pt (1.2 l)
Onion, roughly chopped 1
Carrot, roughly chopped 1
Celery stick, roughly sliced, including leaves 1
Small leek, roughly sliced 1
Fresh herbs, eg bayleaf, sprig of rosemary,
sprig of thyme, parsley stalks

Place all the ingredients in a large saucepan. Slowly bring to the boil and simmer for 15–20 minutes. Strain.
***

QUICK TO MAKE STOCKS

Dissolve a vegetable stock cube (these can be bought either with or without salt) in 1 pt (600 ml) of boiling water to make a light-coloured stock.

Dissolve 1 tsp of vegetable concentrate or yeast extract in 1 pt (600 ml) of boiling water – this makes a dark stock, so be careful to use it in soups where it will not alter the basic colour too much.
***

JAPANESE KOMBU STOCK

Ideal for clear soups where a delicate flavour is
required.

Kombu sea vegetable 4 in (10 cm) (see p. 7)
Dried Japanese or Chinese
mushrooms 2
Water 1½ pt (900 ml)

Soak the kombu and the dried mushrooms in the water
for 10–15 minutes. In a saucepan bring slowly to the
boil. At this point remove from the heat and strain. The
kombu and mushrooms can be used again.

For a stronger flavoured stock, after bringing to the
boil simmer for 5–10 minutes.
***

CLEAR MUSHROOM, CUCUMBER & RADISH SOUP

This is a delicately flavoured and prettily presented Japanese soup using traditional sea vegetables which are highly nutritious and yet quick and simple to use.

Kombu sea vegetable 4 in (10 cm) (see p. 7)
Water 1½ pt (900 ml)
Onion, finely sliced 1
Mushrooms, finely sliced 4 oz (100 g)
Root ginger, roughly chopped, 1 in (2.5 cm)
Soya sauce 1 tbsp (15 ml)
Cucumber, thinly sliced 3 oz (75 g)
Salt to taste
Radish, thinly sliced 2 oz (50 g)
Nori sea vegetable, toasted (see p. 7)
and spring onions, chopped to garnish

Place the kombu in a saucepan and cover with the water. Add the onion and bring gently to boiling point then simmer for 15 minutes. Add the mushrooms and continue simmering for a further 5 minutes. Remove the kombu from the stock (it can be saved and used again for flavouring). Place the ginger in a garlic press and squeeze out the juice. Add to the pan with the soya sauce. Add the cucumber and additional salt if necessary and cook for only two more minutes. The cucumber should become transparent, but still retain its crispness. Place the radish in the serving bowls reserving a few slices for garnish. Ladle the soup over and garnish by floating a piece of nori and sliced radish on the surface and sprinkling with spring onions.

(To prepare the nori garnish: toast lightly by holding one sheet of nori over the hotplate or gas ring. It will very quickly crisp and turn bright green. Cut into 1 in (2.5 cm) squares or strips and set aside).

Serves 4–6

BEETROOT & TOMATO SOUP

The dash of cream or yoghourt is essential for the presentation of this colourful soup.

Oil 1 tbsp (15 ml)
Onion, roughly chopped 1
Raw beetroot, diced 8 oz (225 g)
Garlic cloves, crushed 2
Cumin seeds 1 tsp (5 ml)
Ground cinnamon ¼ tsp (1.25 ml)
Tomatoes, quartered 8 oz (225 g)
Tomato juice ½ pt (300 ml)
Tomato purée 1 tbsp (15 ml)
Vegetable stock 1 pt (600 ml) (see p. 10)
Vegetable stock cube 1
Soya sauce 1 tbsp (15 ml)
Salt & pepper to taste
Soured cream or yoghourt 4 tbsp (60 ml)
Chives or spring onions, chopped to garnish

Heat oil in a large saucepan. Add the onion, beetroot and garlic and cook gently for 5 minutes. Add the cumin seeds and cinnamon and continue cooking for a few more minutes. Next add the tomatoes, tomato juice and tomato purée, then the stock and stock cube. Cover and simmer for 45 minutes or until the vegetables are tender. Purée the soup in a liquidizer or food processor. Add the soya sauce and season to taste. Garnish with soured cream and serve sprinkled with chopped chives or spring onions.

Serves 4
***

CURRIED CREAM
OF PARSNIP SOUP

Butter or margarine 1 oz (25 g)
Medium-sized parsnips, chopped 2
Onion, chopped 1
Potato, diced 1
Root ginger, roughly chopped 1 inch (2.5 cm)
Garlic cloves, crushed 2
Curry powder 2–4 tsp (10–20 ml)
Vegetable stock 1¼ pt (750 ml) (see p. 10)
Vegetable stock cube 1
Milk ½ pt (300 ml)
Salt to taste
Single cream ¼ pt (150 ml)
Coriander or chives, freshly chopped to garnish

Melt the butter or margarine in a saucepan. Add the
parsnips, onion and potato and cook gently for 5
minutes. Put the ginger in a garlic press, squeeze the
juice into the pan then add the garlic and curry powder.
Cook, stirring for 2–3 minutes. Add the stock and stock
cube. Cover and simmer for 30 minutes or until the
vegetables are tender. Allow to cool a little and blend in
a liquidizer or food processor with the milk. Return to
the pan. Adjust the seasoning and add the cream,
reserving a little for garnish. Reheat gently without
boiling. Serve with a swirl of cream and freshly
chopped coriander or chives.

Serves 4
***

CLEAR MUSHROOM & PEPPER SOUP

A colourful oriental-style soup with a light,
fresh flavour.

Vegetable stock 2½ pt (1.5 l) (see p. 10)
Onion, finely sliced 1
Dried thyme ½ tsp (2.5 ml)
Dried tarragon ½ tsp (2.5 ml)
Mushrooms, wiped and sliced 8 oz (225 g)
Red pepper, deseeded and
thinly sliced 1
Green pepper, deseeded and
thinly sliced 1
Soya sauce 1–2 tbsp (15–30 ml)
Salt & pepper to taste
Spring onions, chopped to garnish

Bring the stock, onion and herbs to the boil in a
saucepan. Simmer for 3 minutes. Add the mushrooms
and continue cooking for a further 3 minutes. Add
green and red peppers and simmer for another 2–3
minutes. The peppers should still be a little crisp in the
centre and be brightly coloured. Add the soya sauce
and seasoning to taste. Ladle into bowls and serve
sprinkled with spring onions.

Serves 4–6

SPINACH, TOFU & MISO SOUP

This soup is very easy to make, but be careful not to overcook the vegetables.

Oil 1 tbsp (15 ml)
Onion, finely sliced 1
Carrot, thinly sliced 1
Root ginger, roughly chopped 1 in (2.5 cm)
Garlic clove, crushed 1
Vegetable stock 2½ pt (1.5 l) (see p. 10)
Plain or smoked tofu 8 oz (225 g)
cut into ½ in (1 cm) cubes
Spinach, finely shredded 8 oz (225 g)
Miso 2 tbsp (30 ml) (see p. 6)
Spring onion, chopped to garnish

Heat the oil in a large saucepan. Add the onion and carrot and cook gently for 3 minutes. Place the ginger in a garlic press and squeeze out the juice. Add to the vegetables with the garlic. Add the stock and bring to the boil. Drop in the tofu and allow to boil for 2 minutes. Add the shredded spinach, bring back to the boil and cook only until the spinach has wilted (1–2 minutes – but is still bright green). Meanwhile, blend the miso with a little cold water or stock to a pouring consistency. Remove soup from the heat and stir in the miso. Reheat if necessary but do not allow to boil. Serve immediately, sprinkled with chopped spring onions.

Serves 6

MILLET & ONION SOUP

As an alternative garnish sprinkle with grated cheese
and crisp under the grill – but be sure to use
heat-proof bowls.

Butter or margarine 1 oz (25 g)
Onions, finely sliced 1 lb (450 g)
Salt 1 tsp (5 ml)
Sugar a pinch
Millet 3 oz (75 g)
Bayleaf 1
Vegetable stock 2¾ pt (1.7 l) (see p. 10)
Vegetable stock cube 1
Soya sauce 1 tbsp (15 ml)
Salt & pepper to taste
Spring onions, chopped to garnish

Heat the butter or margarine in a large saucepan, add
the onions, cover and cook on a low heat for 15
minutes. Add the salt and sugar, turn the heat up a little
and cook uncovered for a further 15 minutes stirring
frequently to prevent burning. Meanwhile, dry roast
the millet in a pan over a medium heat until it turns
golden brown and releases a nutty fragrance. Add the
bayleaf, stock and stock cube to the onions and stir in
the roasted millet. Cover and simmer for 30 minutes or
until millet is cooked and the soup slightly thickened.
Add the soya sauce, remove the bayleaf and adjust
seasoning to taste. Sprinkle with chopped spring
onions before serving.

Serves 6
***

CREAM OF HARICOT
BEAN SOUP

For added effect serve this delicately pale-coloured
soup in a dark bowl.

Butter or margarine 1 oz (25 g)
Onion, chopped 1
Small parsnip, diced 1
Leek, sliced 1
Celery stick, sliced 1
Garlic cloves, crushed 2
Dried tarragon 1 tsp (5 ml)
Bayleaf 1
Haricot beans, soaked overnight 8 oz (225 g)
Vegetable stock 1½ pt (900 ml) (see p. 10)
Vegetable stock cube 1
Fresh parsley, chopped 1 tbsp (15 ml)
Milk ½ pt (300 ml)
Salt & pepper to taste
Single cream ¼ pt (150 ml)
Chopped parsley to garnish

Melt the butter or margarine, add the onion, parsnip,
leek, celery and garlic. Cover and cook over a low heat
for 5 minutes. Add the tarragon and bayleaf. Drain and
rinse the haricot beans and add to the vegetables with
the stock and stock cube. Bring to the boil, cover and
simmer for about one hour or until the beans are soft.
Remove the bayleaf and blend in a liquidizer or food
processor until smooth. Add the fresh parsley and
blend in the milk. Season to taste. Return to the pan,
add the cream and reheat without allowing the soup to
boil. Serve sprinkled with chopped parsley.

Serves 4–6
***

CREAM OF CARROT & BARLEY SOUP

Try this unusual soup. The addition of barley makes it especially smooth and creamy.

Butter or margarine 1 oz (25 g)
Onion, roughly chopped 1
Carrots, sliced 1 lb (450 g)
Potato, diced 1
Small turnip, diced 1
Fresh herbs, chopped 1 tbsp (15 ml)
or
Dried mixed herbs 1 tsp (5 ml)
Vegetable stock 2 pt (1.2 l) (see p. 10)
Vegetable stock cube 1
Pot barley 2 oz (50 g)
Milk ½ pt (300 ml)
Single cream ¼ pt (150 ml)
Salt & pepper to taste
Chopped chives to garnish

Melt the butter or margarine in a large saucepan and add the onion, carrots, potato, turnip and herbs. Cover and cook gently for 5 minutes. Then add the stock, stock cube and barley. Simmer the soup for 45 minutes or until the barley is tender (though it will remain fairly chewy). Allow to cool a little and blend in a liquidizer or food processor. Return the soup to the pan and add the milk and cream, reserving a little for garnishing. Season to taste and reheat carefully without boiling. Serve with a swirl of cream and chopped chives.

Serves 4–6
***

MINESTRONE SOUP WITH MISO

The use of miso enriches the flavour of this traditional
Italian soup.

Haricot beans, soaked overnight 2 oz (50 g)
Vegetable stock 2½ pt (1.5 l) (see p. 10)
Oil 2 tbsp (30 ml)
Onion, sliced 1
Celery stick, sliced 1
Carrot, diced 1
Garlic cloves, crushed 2
Leek, sliced 1
Fresh oregano, chopped 1 tbsp (15 ml)
Fresh basil, chopped 1 tbsp (15 ml)
Tomatoes, quartered 8 oz (225 g)
Tomato purée 1 tbsp (15 ml)
Bayleaf 1
Cauliflower florets 4 oz (100 g)
Wholewheat pasta 2 oz (50 g)
Miso 1 tbsp (15 ml) (see p. 6)
Salt & pepper to taste
Freshly grated Parmesan cheese
and chopped parsley to garnish

Drain and rinse the beans, place in a pan with 1 pt (600
ml) of the stock. Bring to the boil, cover and simmer
gently for 30 minutes. Heat the oil in a large saucepan
and add the onion, celery and carrot. Cover and cook
gently for 5 minutes. Add the garlic, leek and herbs and
cook for a few more minutes. Add the remaining stock,
tomatoes, tomato purée, bayleaf, cooked beans in their
stock. Simmer for a further 15 minutes. Add the
cauliflower florets and wholewheat pasta and continue
cooking until these are just tender. Remove the pan
from the heat. Blend the miso with a little cold water in
a small basin to make a thin paste. Gradually stir into
the soup. Season to taste. (Take care when adding salt
as miso is naturally quite salty). Serve, garnished with
cheese and chopped parsley.

Serves 4–6   20
***

MEXICAN BROTH

This substantial hot soup is a meal in itself. Serve it with crusty bread and a crisp green salad.

Oil 1 tbsp (15 ml)
Onion, thinly sliced 1
Dried basil ½ tsp (2.5 ml)
Dried thyme ½ tsp (2.5 ml)
Garlic cloves, crushed 2
Red kidney beans (see p. 6) soaked overnight 4 oz (100 g)
Vegetable stock 2½ pt (1.5 l) (see p. 10)
Vegetable stock cube 1
Bayleaf 1
Brown rice 2 oz (50 g)
Celery stick, sliced 1
Leek, sliced 1
Tomatoes, quartered 8 oz (225 g)
Red wine, optional ¼ pt (150 ml)
Chilli powder ¼ tsp (1.25 ml)
Red pepper, deseeded & thinly sliced 1
Green pepper, deseeded & thinly sliced 1
Soya sauce 1 tbsp (15 ml)
Salt & pepper to taste
Freshly chopped parsley to garnish

Heat the oil in a large saucepan. Sauté the onions, herbs and garlic for 5 minutes until transparent. Drain the red kidney beans and add to the saucepan with the stock, stock cube and the bayleaf. Cover and cook vigorously for 15 minutes, then simmer for a further 30 minutes or until the beans are tender. Add the rice, celery, leek, tomatoes and the red wine if using. Cover and cook for a further 25 minutes. Add the sliced peppers and the soya sauce. Season to taste. Cook for 3 more minutes to soften the peppers a little but do not overcook or they will lose their bright colour. Sprinkle with chopped parsley before serving.

Serves 4–6
***

ICED CHICKPEA, CUCUMBER & YOGHOURT SOUP

A lovely summer soup – try it for a picnic.

Chickpeas, soaked overnight 6 oz (175 g)
Garlic cloves, crushed 2
Cucumber, finely chopped 1
Lemon juice 2 tbsp (30 ml)
Fresh mint, finely chopped 2 tbsp (30 ml)
Natural yoghourt 1 pt (600 ml)
Salt & pepper to taste
Ice cubes and freshly chopped mint to garnish

Drain and rinse the chickpeas. Cover with fresh water, add the garlic. Simmer until tender, 45 minutes–1 hour or approximately 15–20 minutes in a pressure cooker at 15 lb (7 kg) pressure. Drain, reserving the liquid. Blend the cooked chickpeas with 1–1½ pt (600 ml–900 ml) of the reserved liquid in a liquidizer or food processor. Add the remaining ingredients, stir well. Season to taste and chill. Serve garnished with ice cubes and sprinkled with chopped mint.

Serves 6

BUTTERBEAN & TOMATO SOUP

Any white beans can be used as an alternative to
butterbeans.

Butter or margarine 1 oz (25 g)
Onion, roughly chopped 1
Bayleaf 1
Dried basil ½ tsp (2.5 ml)
Dried thyme ½ tsp (2.5 ml)
Tomato juice ½ pt (300 ml)
Tomato purée 1 tbsp (15 ml)
Tomatoes, sliced 8 oz (225 g)
Vegetable stock 1 pt (600 ml) (see p. 10)
Vegetable stock cube 1
Butterbeans, soaked overnight 4 oz (100 g)
Soya sauce 1 tbsp (15 ml)
Salt & pepper to taste
Chives, chopped to garnish

Melt the butter or margarine in a large saucepan and
add the onion and herbs. Cook gently until transparent.
Add the tomato juice, tomato purée, tomatoes, stock
and stock cube. Drain the butterbeans and add to the
saucepan. Bring to the boil, cover and simmer for about
50 minutes or until the beans are tender. Remove the
bayleaf. Allow to cool a little and blend the soup until
smooth in a liquidizer or food processor. Add the soya
sauce and adjust the seasoning to taste. Serve sprinkled
with chopped chives.

Serves 4–6
***

CREAM OF CAULIFLOWER SOUP

Butter or margarine 1 oz (25 g)
Onion, chopped 1
Potato, diced 1
Cauliflower, broken into florets 1
Vegetable stock 1½ pt (900 ml) (see p. 10)
Ground nutmeg (a pinch)
Milk ½ pt (300 ml)
Salt & pepper to taste
Single cream 2 fl oz (50 ml)
Chopped parsley to garnish

Melt the butter or margarine in a large saucepan. Add the onion, potato and cauliflower reserving a few small florets for garnish. Cover and cook gently for 5 minutes, stirring occasionally. Add the stock, cover and simmer for about 15 minutes or until the vegetables are tender. Meanwhile, blanch the reserved cauliflower florets in boiling water for 2 minutes. Drain and set aside.

Blend the soup in a liquidizer or food processor until smooth. Return to the pan with the nutmeg and milk. Season to taste. Stir in the cream and gently reheat without allowing to boil. Serve garnished with blanched cauliflower florets and chopped parsley.

Serves 4–6
***

CARROT & ORANGE SOUP

A versatile soup which may be served hot or cold.

Butter or margarine 1 oz (25 g)
Onion, roughly chopped 1
Carrots, diced 1 lb (450 g)
Potato, diced 1
Dried chervil 1 tsp (5 ml)
Vegetable stock 1½ pt (900 ml) (see p. 10)
Orange, juice of 1
Salt & pepper to taste
Single cream 4 tbsp (60 ml)
Chives, chopped to garnish

Melt the butter or margarine in a large saucepan. Add the onion, carrots, potato and chervil and toss in the butter. Cover and cook gently for 5 minutes without allowing to brown. Add the stock and simmer for about 30 minutes or until vegetables are tender.

Allow to cool a little and blend the soup in a liquidizer or food processor and add the orange juice and season to taste with salt and pepper. Return to the pan with half of the cream and reheat without allowing to boil. Serve, swirling the remaining cream over the surface and sprinkle with chopped chives.

VARIATION
For a refreshing summer soup, chill after puréeing then add ¼ pt (150 ml) natural yoghourt. Serve with ice cubes and fresh mint.

Serves 4–6
***

PUMPKIN, TARRAGON & COCONUT SOUP

Try this unusual autumn soup when the pumpkins are plentiful – the coconut gives it a creamy texture.

Pumpkin, peeled, deseeded & chopped 1 lb (450 g)
Carrot, diced 1
Dried tarragon 1 tsp (5 ml)
Vegetable stock 2 pt (1.2 l) (see p. 10)
Coconut milk powder 2 tbsp (30 ml) (see p. 6)
or creamed coconut 2 oz (50 g)
Salt & pepper to taste
Freshly chopped chives or tarragon to garnish

Place the pumpkin, carrot and tarragon in a large saucepan. Cover with the stock and bring to the boil. Cover and simmer for 30 minutes until vegetables are tender. Allow to cool and blend in a liquidizer or food processor. Blend in the coconut milk powder or creamed coconut and season to taste. To serve, reheat gently and sprinkle with freshly chopped chives or tarragon.

Serves 4–6
***

YELLOW SPLIT PEA, PARSNIP & LEMON SOUP

Butter or margarine 1 oz (25 g)
Onion, chopped 1
Medium-sized parsnips, diced 2
Celery stick, sliced 1
Medium-sized potato, diced 1
Garlic clove, crushed 1
Cumin seeds 1 tsp (5 ml)
Yellow split peas, soaked overnight 4 oz (100 g)
Vegetable stock 2½ pt (1.5 l) (see p. 10)
Vegetable stock cube 1
Parsley, chopped 1 tbsp (15 ml)
Lemon, juice of ½
Salt & pepper to taste
Paprika and freshly chopped parsley to garnish

Heat the butter or margarine in a large saucepan. Add the onion, parsnip, celery, potato, garlic and cumin seeds and cook gently for 5 minutes. Drain and rinse the split peas and add to the pan with the stock and stock cube. Bring to the boil, cover and simmer until tender, approximately 45 minutes. Allow to cool a little before blending the soup in a liquidizer or food processor until smooth. Add the parsley, lemon juice and seasoning to taste. Reheat and serve sprinkled with paprika and freshly chopped parsley.

VARIATION
To make a Cream of Split Pea and Parsnip soup, add 2 fl oz (50 ml) single cream in place of the lemon juice.

Serves 4–6
***

CREAM OF MUSHROOM & LENTIL SOUP

Red lentils were used in this dark mushroom soup, but brown or green could be substituted. However, they will require slightly longer cooking.

Butter or margarine 1 oz (25 g)
Onion, chopped 1
Mushrooms, sliced 8 oz (225 g)
Garlic clove, crushed 1
Dried thyme ½ tsp (2.5 ml)
Dried oregano ½ tsp (2.5 ml)
Bayleaf 1
Red lentils, washed 4 oz (100 g)
Vegetable stock 1½ pt (900 ml) (see p. 10)
Vegetable stock cube 1
Milk ¼ pt (150 ml)
Salt & pepper to taste
Single cream 2 fl oz (50 ml)
Chopped parsley to garnish

Melt the butter or margarine in a large saucepan and cook the onion gently until transparent. Add the mushrooms, garlic, and herbs and continue cooking for a further 2–3 minutes. Then add the lentils, stock and stock cube. Bring to the boil, cover and simmer for 20 minutes or until the lentils are soft. Allow to cool slightly. Remove the bayleaf and blend the soup in a liquidizer or food processor. Add the milk and season to taste. Add the cream and reheat gently without allowing to boil. Serve sprinkled with chopped parsley.

Serves 4–6
***

COURGETTE, TOMATO & WALNUT SOUP

Walnuts give this soup an extra crunchy texture.

Oil 1 tbsp (15 ml)
Onion, finely chopped 1
Potato, diced 1
Garlic clove, crushed 1
Tomatoes, roughly chopped 12 oz (350 g)
Tomato juice ½ pt (300 ml)
Vegetable stock 1½ pt (900 ml) (see p. 10)
Vegetable stock cube 1
Bayleaf 1
Dried oregano ½ tsp (2.5 ml)
Courgettes, sliced 1 lb (450 g)
Fresh basil, chopped 1 tbsp (15 ml)
Chopped walnuts 2 oz (50 g)
Salt & pepper to taste
Fresh basil to garnish

Heat the oil in a large saucepan. Add the onion, potato and garlic and sauté for 5 minutes without browning. Add the tomatoes, tomato juice, vegetable stock, stock cube, bayleaf, and oregano. Bring to the boil, cover and simmer until the vegetables are cooked, about 20 minutes. Add the courgettes and basil and continue cooking for a further 5 minutes. Stir in the chopped walnuts and season to taste. Garnish with fresh basil.

Serves 4–6
***

BROWN RICE & GINGER SOUP

This is an excellent way of using up left-over cooked rice. Make it by substituting 8 oz (225 g) cooked brown rice and reducing the cooking time slightly.

Japanese kombu stock, 1 quantity,
reserving mushrooms (see p. 11)
Onion, finely chopped 1
Brown rice 8 oz (225 g)
Celery stick, finely sliced 1
Root ginger, roughly chopped 1 in (2.5 cm)
Soya sauce 1 tbsp (15 ml)
Salt & pepper to taste
Sherry dry or medium 1 tbsp (15 ml)
Honey 2 tsp (10 ml)
Chopped spring onion & diced
red pepper to garnish

Reserve the mushrooms from the stock. Discard the stalks and slice the cap. Pour the stock into a saucepan. Add the onion, rice and celery, cover and simmer gently for 40 minutes. Place the ginger in a garlic press and squeeze out the juice. Add to the pan with the soya sauce and adjust seasoning if necessary. Add the sherry and honey and serve sprinkled with spring onion and red pepper.

Serves 4–6

CHICK PEA BROTH

Chick peas, soaked overnight 4 oz (100 g)
Oil 1 tbsp (15 ml)
Garlic clove, crushed 1
Onion, finely chopped 1
Carrot, thinly sliced 1
Medium-sized parsnip, diced 1
Chilli powder (or to taste) ¼ tsp (1.25 ml)
Vegetable stock approx 2 pt (1.2 l) (see p. 10)
Vegetable stock cubes 2
Tomatoes, quartered 12 oz (350 g)
Tomato juice ½ pt (300 ml)
Bayleaf 1
Dried thyme 1 tsp (5 ml)
Celery stick, sliced 1
Green pepper, deseeded and sliced 1
Soya sauce 1 tbsp (15 ml)
Salt & pepper to taste
Freshly chopped parsley to garnish

Drain and rinse the chick peas. Cover with water and cook until tender, 45 minutes–1 hour or 15–20 minutes in a pressure cooker at 15 lb (7 kg) pressure. Drain, reserving the liquid. Heat the oil in a large saucepan. Add the garlic, onion, carrot and parsnip. Cover and cook gently for 5 minutes. Add the chilli powder and cook for another minute. Make the reserved chick pea liquid up to 2 pts (1.2 l) with water and add to the pan with the stock cubes, tomatoes, tomato juice, bayleaf and thyme. Add the drained chick peas, cover and cook for about 20 minutes or until the vegetables are tender.

Add the celery, green pepper, soya sauce and seasoning and continue cooking for 5 minutes, remove the bayleaf. Finally, stir in the freshly chopped parsley just before serving.

Serves 6
***

CHILLED APRICOT & ORANGE SOUP

A delicate fruit flavour makes this summer vegetable soup quite special.

Butter or margarine 1 oz (25 g)
Onion, chopped 1
Potato, diced 1
Carrot, diced 1
Dried chervil 1 tsp (5 ml)
Dried apricots, soaked overnight 4 oz (100 g)
Vegetable stock 1½ pt (900 ml) (see p. 10)
Vegetable stock cube 1
Orange 1
Soya sauce 1 tbsp (15 ml)
Salt & pepper to taste
Natural yoghourt ½ pt (300 ml)
Chives or spring onions, chopped to garnish

Heat the butter or margarine in a saucepan. Add the onion, potato, carrot and chervil, cover and cook gently for 5 minutes. Add the apricots, with their liquid and the vegetable stock and stock cube. Cover the pan and allow to simmer gently for 30 minutes. Leave to cool slightly. Blend until smooth in a liquidizer or food processor. Add the grated rind of ½ of the orange and all the juice. Season with the soya sauce and salt and pepper to taste. Chill throroughly. To serve, blend in the natural yoghourt to make a smooth soup and garnish with chopped chives or spring onions.

Serves 4–6
***

SWEET & SOUR CABBAGE & APPLE SOUP

Butter or margarine 1 oz (25 g)
Onion, finely diced 1
Celery stick, thinly sliced 1
Potato, diced 1
Root ginger, roughly chopped 1 in (2.5 cm)
Garlic clove, crushed 1
Cooking apple, cored and finely diced 8 oz (225 g)
Vegetable stock 3 pt (1.8 l) (see p. 10)
Vegetable stock cubes 2
Bayleaf 1
Tomatoes, chopped 8 oz (225 g)
Apple concentrate 1 tbsp (15 ml) (see p. 5)
Cider vinegar 2 tsp (10 ml)
Cabbage, finely shredded 10 oz (275 g)
Soya sauce 2 tbsp (30 ml)
Salt & pepper to taste
Soured cream or natural yoghourt
& chopped spring onions to garnish

Melt the butter or margarine in a large saucepan. Add the onion, celery and potato, cover and cook gently for 5 minutes. Put the ginger in a garlic press, squeeze out the juice and add to the pan with the garlic. Add the apple and sauté for a further 2 minutes. Next add the stock and stock cubes, bayleaf, tomatoes, apple concentrate and cider vinegar. Bring to the boil and add the cabbage. Simmer for 5–7 minutes until the cabbage is just tender. Remove the bayleaf, add the soya sauce and adjust seasoning to taste. Serve with soured cream and chopped spring onion to garnish.

Note: If wished, the soup may be blended before serving.

Serves 6
***

CREAM OF TOMATO & CAULIFLOWER SOUP

Butter or margarine 1 oz (25 g)
Onion, diced 1
Garlic clove, crushed 1
Medium-sized potato, diced 1
Small cauliflower, broken into florets 1
Tomatoes, chopped 8 oz (225 g)
Vegetable stock 1 pt (600 ml) (see p. 10)
Vegetable stock cube 1
Tomato juice ½ pt (300 ml)
Tomato purée 1 tbsp (15 ml)
Bayleaf 1
Dried mixed herbs ½ tsp (2.5 ml)
Dried oregano ½ tsp (2.5 ml)
Freshly chopped basil 1 tbsp (15 ml)
Milk ½ pt (300 ml)
Salt & pepper to taste
Single cream 2 fl oz (50 ml)
Fresh basil to garnish

Melt the butter or margarine in a large saucepan. Add the onion, garlic, potato and cauliflower (reserving a few florets for garnish). Toss well in the butter then lower the heat and cook for 5 minutes then add the tomatoes, stock and stock cube, tomato juice, tomato purée, bayleaf, mixed herbs and oregano. Cover and simmer for 20 minutes or until the vegetables are cooked. Add the fresh basil and remove the bayleaf. Allow to cool a little. Blend until smooth in a liquidizer or food processor. Return the soup to the saucepan. Add the milk and season to taste.

Add the cream and reheat without boiling. Serve garnished with tiny cauliflower florets that have been blanched in boiling water for 1 minute, and a small leaf of fresh basil.

Serves 4–6
***

CURRIED AVOCADO SOUP

This soup may be served hot or chilled. When serving it hot, a little less lemon juice and spice is needed, as heating brings out these flavours. It must be served immediately, to avoid losing its colour.

Vegetable stock 1½ pt (900 ml) (see p. 10)
Vegetable stock cube 1
Onion, diced 1
Garlic clove, crushed 1
Curry powder 2 tsp (10 ml)
Avocado 2
Lemon juice 1 tbsp (15 ml)
Soya sauce 1 tbsp (15 ml)
Chopped parsley 1 tbsp (15 ml)
Single cream or natural yoghourt 2 fl oz (50 ml)
Parsley to garnish

Heat the vegetable stock, stock cube, onion, garlic and curry powder in a saucepan. Bring to the boil and simmer for 5 minutes or until the onion is soft. Just before using, scoop the flesh from the avocado and combine in a liquidizer or food processor with the lemon juice, soya sauce and chopped parsley. Gradually add the cooled curry stock and blend until smooth. Add a little more liquid if the soup is too thick. Add the single cream or yoghourt and either heat very gently without allowing to boil and serve immediately, or chill and serve cold.

Serves 4

CREAMY ONION SOUP

Butter or margarine 2 oz (50 g)
Medium-sized onion, finely chopped 2
Bayleaf 1
Dried sage ¹/₂ tsp (2.5 ml)
Dried thyme ¹/₂ tsp (2.5 ml)
Dried marjoram ¹/₂ tsp (2.5 ml)
Ground ginger, a pinch
Small potato, diced 1
Medium carrot, grated 1
Vegetable stock or water 1 pt (600 ml) (see p. 10)
Vegetable stock cube 1
Red wine or port (30 ml)
Soya sauce 1 tsp (5 ml)
Milk ¹/₄ pt (150 ml)
Parsley, chopped 1 tbsp (15 ml)
Salt & pepper to taste
Cream to garnish

Melt the butter or margarine in a large saucepan. Add the finely chopped onion, the bayleaf, sage, thyme, marjoram and ginger. Cover and sauté gently for about 10 minutes until transparent and glossy, but do not allow to brown. Add the diced potato and grated carrot reserving a little for garnish. Add the stock, stock cube, red wine and soya sauce. Cover and simmer until tender, approximately 20 minutes. Remove the bayleaf, allow to cool, then blend in a liquidizer or food processor until smooth.

Blend in the milk. Return to the pan and reheat. Stir in the chopped parsley and season to taste. Serve garnished with a swirl of cream and the reserved grated carrot for a dash of colour.

Serves 4–6
***

SHERRIED SWEDE & BARLEY SOUP

This delicious soup is enhanced by the addition of a touch of orange juice.

Butter or margarine 1 oz (25 g)
Onion, roughly chopped 1
Swede, roughly chopped 1 lb (450 g)
Sherry, dry or medium 2 tbsp (30 ml)
Orange, finely grated rind 1½ tsp (7.5 ml)
Vegetable stock 2 pt (1.2 l) (see p. 10)
Vegetable stock cube 1
Pot barley 3 oz (75 g)
Bayleaf 1
Orange juice 3 tbsp (45 ml)
Salt & pepper to taste
Orange rind, blanched and shredded to garnish

Melt the butter or margarine in a large saucepan. Add the onion, swede, sherry and grated orange rind and cook over a medium heat for 5 minutes. Take care not to brown the vegetables, but the liquid should be reduced by half. Next add the stock and stock cube, the pot barley and the bayleaf. Cover and cook until the barley is tender, about 45 minutes. Allow to cool slightly. Remove the bayleaf and blend the soup in a liquidizer or food processor, adding the orange juice. Season to taste and serve garnished with finely shredded orange rind that has been blanched in boiling water for 1 minute.

Serves 4–6
***

VICHYSSOISE WITH WATERCRESS

Based on a simple leek and potato soup made in many
French homes, Vichyssoise, served chilled with the
addition of cream, has become a classic. This version is
made with watercress. Yoghourt can be used as an
alternative to cream. It is just as delicious served hot.

Butter or margarine 2 oz (50 g)
Leeks, roughly chopped 1 lb (450 g)
Potatoes, roughly chopped 1 lb (450 g)
Vegetable stock 3 pt (1.8 l) (see p. 10)
Salt & pepper to taste
Watercress 1 bunch
Single cream or natural yoghourt ¼ pt (150 ml)
Chopped chives or watercress to garnish

Melt the butter or margarine in a large saucepan. Add
the leeks and potato, coating well with the fat. Cover
and cook gently for 5 minutes without browning. Add
the stock and simmer until the vegetables are tender,
about 15 minutes. Let the soup cool for a few minutes,
then blend in a liquidizer or food processor, adding the
watercress. Season to taste. Chill thoroughly then add
the cream or yoghourt before serving, or reheat gently
without boiling. Serve garnished with chives or
watercress.

Serves 6
***

GARLIC HERB SOUP

Don't be put off by the quantity of garlic – try it!
It's remarkably mild and smooth.

Garlic cloves 16–30
Vegetable stock 2½ pt (1.5 l) (see p. 10)
Olive oil 3 tbsp (45 ml)
Freshly chopped parsley 1 tbsp (15 ml)
Bayleaf 1
Dried thyme ¼ tsp (1.25 ml)
Dried sage ¼ tsp (1.25 ml)
Salt & pepper to taste
Egg yolks 3
Chopped parsley & wholemeal croutons to garnish

Pour boiling water over the garlic cloves, leave to soak
for 1 minute, drain and peel. Place in a large saucepan
with the stock, oil and herbs. Bring to the boil and
simmer for 45 minutes. Cool slightly then blend in a
liquidizer or food processor. Return to the pan and
season to taste. Pour a little of the warm liquid over the
egg yolks and blend until smooth. Add to the soup,
stirring constantly and heat very gently until it thickens
slightly. Do not allow the soup to boil or it will curdle.
Serve immediately, garnished with chopped parsley
and wholemeal croutons (see p. 75).

Serves 6
***

39

CREAM OF BROCCOLI & ALMOND SOUP

Butter or margarine 1 oz (25 g)
Onion, roughly chopped 1
Garlic clove, crushed 1
Medium-sized potato, diced 1
Broccoli, cut into small pieces 1 lb (450 g)
Vegetable stock 1¼ pt (750 ml) (see p. 10)
Vegetable stock cube 1
Milk ½ pt (300 ml)
Whole blanched almonds or flaked
almonds, toasted 2 oz (50 g)
Ground nutmeg, a pinch
Salt & pepper to taste
Single cream 2 fl oz (50 ml)
Parsley and toasted flaked almonds to garnish

Melt the butter or margarine in a saucepan and add the onion, garlic, potato and broccoli. Toss well in the butter then leave to cook without browning for 5 minutes. Add the stock and stock cube, cover and simmer until the vegetables are tender, about 15 minutes. Add the milk and almonds. Blend until smooth in a liquidizer or food processor. Season with nutmeg and salt and pepper. Add the cream and reheat gently without boiling. Serve garnished with parsley and flaked almonds.

Serves 4–6
***

Clear mushroom & pepper soup, page 15
Courgette tomato & walnut soup, page 29
Spinach, tofu & miso soup, page 16

Millet & onion soup, page 17
Beetroot & tomato soup, page 13
Pumpkin, tarragon & coconut soup, page 26

Caribbean pepperpot, page 43
Mexican broth, page 21
Chickpea broth, page 31

Carrot & orange soup, page 25
Chilled apricot & orange soup, page 32
Iced chickpea, cucumber & yoghourt soup, page 22

Spicy avocado & pineapple dip, page 82
Mushrooms with white wine & rosemary, page 45
Asparagus in orange sauce, page 49

Alsace onion tartlets, page 58
Green peppercorn sauce, page 79
Rainbow terrine, page 61
Spicy lentil patties, page 67

Spicy onion fritters with yoghourt herb sauce, page 53
Sesame shrouded leeks with tomato sauce, page 65
Carrot stuffed avocados, page 68

Stop-go salad, page 57
Exotic salad starter, page 57
Iced tomato crush, page 73

STILTON SOUP

Serve this cheesy soup with hot crusty bread.

Butter or margarine 1 oz (25 g)
Medium-sized onions, roughly chopped 2
Potatoes, diced 1 lb (450 g)
Bayleaf 1
Vegetable stock 1½ pt (900 ml) (see p. 10)
Vegetable stock cube 1
Chopped parsley 2 tbsp (30 ml)
Stilton cheese 4 oz (100 g)
Salt & pepper to taste
Parsley or chopped chives to garnish

Heat the butter or margarine in a saucepan. Add the
onions and potato, cover and cook gently for 5 minutes.
Add the bayleaf, vegetable stock and stock cube. Cover
and simmer until tender, about 15 minutes. Cool the
soup a little, remove the bayleaf and purée the soup in a
liquidizer or food processor adding the parsley and
crumbled stilton. Season to taste and serve garnished
with chopped parsley or chives.

Serves 4–6
***

CELERY & CHEESE SOUP

Butter or margarine 1 oz (25 g)
Medium-sized onion roughly chopped 1
Celery, a head, sliced
approx. 1 lb (450 g)
Medium-sized potato, diced 1
Vegetable stock 1½ pt (900 ml) (see p. 10)
Vegetable stock cube 1
Cottage cheese 4 oz (100 g)
Salt & pepper to taste
Chopped parsley or celery leaf to garnish

Melt the butter or margarine in a large saucepan. Add
the onion, celery and potato. Cover and cook gently for
5 minutes. Add the stock and the stock cube. Simmer
for 15–20 minutes or until the vegetables are tender.
Allow to cool. Purée the soup in a liquidizer or food
processor with the cheese until smooth. Season to taste.
Return to the pan, and reheat gently without boiling.
Serve garnished with chopped parsley or celery leaves.

Serves 4–6
***

CARIBBEAN PEPPERPOT

Cranks variation of this hot and spicy soup from the Caribbean is popular for chilly evenings. It retains its tropical flavour with a delicate hint of coconut.

Oil 2 tbsp (30 ml)
Medium-sized onion, finely chopped 1
Garlic clove, crushed 1
Medium-sized potato, diced 1
Dried thyme 1 tsp (5 ml)
Chilli powder ¼ tsp (1.25 ml)
Vegetable stock 1¾ pt (1 l) (see p. 10)
Vegetable stock cube 1
Cabbage, shredded 4 oz (100 g)
Red pepper, deseeded and sliced 1
Spinach, finely shredded 8 oz (225 g)
Coconut milk powder 3 tbsp (45 ml)
or creamed coconut 2 oz (50 g) (see p. 6)
Salt & pepper to taste
Chopped spring onions to garnish

Heat the oil in a large saucepan. Add the onion, garlic and potato and cook gently for 5 minutes. Add the thyme and chilli powder and stir into the vegetables. Add the stock, stock cube and cabbage and cook until tender, about 10 minutes. Add the red pepper and spinach and continue cooking for just 2 more minutes. Blend the coconut milk powder in a bowl with a little of the hot soup, then stir it, or the creamed coconut into the pot. Season to taste and serve sprinkled with chopped spring onions.

Serves 4–6
***

FLAGEOLET BEAN &
LEEK POTAGE

Serve this soup piping hot to cheer up a cold winter's
day or chilled with yoghourt for a lovely refreshing
summer starter.

Oil 2 tbsp (30 ml)
Medium-sized onion, chopped 1
Garlic clove, crushed 1
Leeks, sliced 12 oz (350 g)
Dried chervil 1 tsp (5 ml)
Flageolet beans, soaked overnight 4 oz (100 g)
Vegetable stock 1½ pt (900 ml) (see p. 10)
Vegetable stock cube 1
Chopped parsley 2 tbsp (30 ml)
Salt & pepper to taste
Natural yoghourt (optional) ¼ pt (150 ml)
Chopped parsley to garnish

Heat the oil in a large saucepan. Add the onion, garlic,
leeks and chervil, cover and cook gently for 5 minutes.
Add the drained flageolet beans, stock and stock cube.
Bring to the boil, cover and simmer for about one hour
or until beans are tender. Blend in a liquidizer or food
processor, adding the parsley. Season to taste. For a
sharper flavour, stir in the natural yoghourt.

Serves 4–6
***

TZATZIKI

Cucumber, finely diced 4 oz (100 g)
Onion or spring onion, finely chopped 1 tbsp (15 ml)
Fresh mint, finely chopped 2 tbsp (30 ml)
Small garlic clove, crushed 1
Natural yoghourt ½ pt (300 ml)
Salt, pepper & paprika to taste

Mix all the ingredients together and chill until required.
Serve with warm bread or toast, or slices of avocado.

Serves 4

MUSHROOMS WITH WHITE WINE & ROSEMARY

Serve this ever popular starter with Cranks hot garlic
buttered bread (see p. 74).

Butter or margarine 2 oz (50 g)
Onion, thinly sliced 1
Mushrooms, button or sliced 1 lb (450 g)
Dried rosemary 1 tsp (5 ml)
Dry white wine ¼ pt (150 ml)
Salt & pepper to taste
Chopped spring onion or parsley to garnish

Heat the butter or margarine in a large saucepan and
sauté the onions for 2 minutes without browning. Add
the mushrooms and rosemary. Cover and cook gently
to extract the juice from the mushrooms. Add the wine
and boil uncovered to reduce to a syrupy glaze. Season
to taste and serve garnished with spring onions or
parsley.

Serves 4–6

GLAZED ARAME WITH CUCUMBER & RADISH

Cucumber, thinly sliced 8 oz (225 g)
Salt 1 tsp (5 ml)
Arame, soaked for 20 minutes 1 oz (25 g) (see p. 7)
Oil 2 tbsp (30 ml)

SAUCE
Lemon, juice of 1
Root ginger, roughly chopped ½ in (1 cm)
Tomato juice ¼ pt (150 ml)
Garlic clove, crushed 1
Apple concentrate 1 tsp (5 ml) (see p. 5)
or unrefined brown sugar 1 tsp (5 ml)
Arrowroot 1 tsp (5 ml)
Spring onions, chopped 2 tbsp (30 ml)
Radish, sliced 6
Spring onions and radish to garnish

Place the cucumber in a colander and stand it over a bowl. Sprinkle with salt, cover with a saucer and place a weight on top. Leave to stand for 3–4 hours. Rinse the salt off the cucumber and pat dry. Drain the arame, reserving the soaking water. Heat the oil in a saucepan. Add the drained arame and sauté lightly for 5 minutes. Add the cucumber slices and cook quickly.

Place the lemon juice in a small saucepan. Squeeze the ginger in a garlic press to extract the juice and add to the pan. Add the tomato juice, crushed garlic and the sweetener. Blend the arrowroot with a little of the reserved water. Bring the sauce ingredients to the boil then add the arrowroot, stirring until thickened.

Add the sliced radishes to the arame and cucumber mixture and continue cooking for two minutes. Turn into a serving dish. Pour over the sweet-and-sour sauce and garnish with radish and spring onions.

Serves 4–6

CHESTNUT & MUSHROOM PATÉ

Butter 1 oz (25 g)
Mushrooms, roughly chopped 1½ lb (675 g)
Fresh sage, chopped 1 tsp (5 ml)
Garlic clove, crushed 1
Chestnut purée 15.5 oz can (439 g can)
Fresh wholemeal breadcrumbs 2 oz (50 g)
Soya sauce 1 tbsp (15 ml)
Lemon juice 1 tbsp (15 ml)
Brandy 2 tsp (10 ml)
Ground nutmeg a pinch
Chilli powder a pinch
Chives chopped 1 tbsp (15 ml)
Salt & pepper to taste

Melt the butter and sauté the mushrooms until golden, with the sage and garlic. Remove the mushrooms from the pan, draining well, then reduce the liquid to a syrupy glaze. Place all the ingredients, except the chives, in a liquidizer or food processor and purée until fairly smooth. Add chives and season to taste. Chill until required. Serve with warm toast and a salad garnish.

Serves 10–12

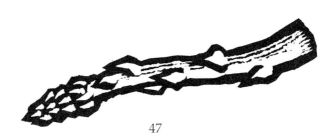

47

AUBERGINE MOUSSE WITH TARRAGON CREAM SAUCE

This is a rich, though delicately flavoured mousse.
Serve it with fingers of wholemeal toast.

Large aubergine 1 (about 1 lb (450 g)
Oil 1 tbsp (15 ml)
Butter or margarine 1 oz (25 g)
Small onion, diced 1
Garlic clove, crushed 1
Dried tarragon 1 tsp (5 ml)
White wine, dry 2 fl oz (50 ml)
Free-range eggs, beaten 2
Whipping cream ¼ pt (150 ml)
Milk 3 fl oz (75 ml)
Salt & pepper to taste
Tarragon cream sauce 1 quantity (see p. 78)
Watercress to garnish

Cut the aubergine in half lengthways, sprinkle with salt
and set aside for 30 minutes to extract the bitter juices.
Rinse and pat dry. Brush with oil and bake in the oven
at 350°F/130°C/gas mark 4 for about 45 minutes or until
flesh is soft. Allow to cool then scoop out the flesh,
discarding the skins. Melt the butter in a saucepan and
sauté the onion and garlic until transparent. Add the
tarragon and white wine and simmer to reduce to half
the volume. In a liquidizer or food processor, blend the
aubergine flesh with the onion mixture until smooth.
Add the beaten eggs, cream and milk and season with
salt and pepper. Pour into six buttered ramekin dishes
or oven-proof moulds. Place in a roasting tin and pour
hot water around. Bake for 20–30 minutes at 400°F/
200°C/gas mark 6 or until set and slightly golden.

To serve, allow the mousse to stand for a couple of
minutes before gently easing it away from the tops of
the dishes. Turn out on to individual plates and finish
with a spoonful of sauce and the watercress.

Serves 6

ASPARAGUS IN ORANGE SAUCE

Nothing could make a more elegant starter when asparagus is in season. However, frozen or canned may be successfully substituted if fresh is unavailable.

Asparagus 1½ lb (675 g)
Oranges 2
White wine 3 fl oz (75 ml)
Butter 1 oz (25 g)
Single cream ¼ pt (150 ml)
Salt & pepper to taste
Orange slices and parsley sprigs to garnish

Remove any woody fibres from the thick ends of the asparagus by carefully peeling to about half-way up the stems. Lower gently into a large pan of boiling salted water and cook until tender, about 5–10 minutes. (There is no need to tie into bundles or stand upright in water, as peeling should ensure the tops and stems cook in the same time. Do take care not to overcook though, as the flavour, texture and colour will be lost.)

Meanwhile prepare the sauce. Wash the oranges. Using a sharp knife remove the peel from half an orange making sure there is no pith. Shred finely then blanch in boiling water for 1 minute. Drain and set aside. Squeeze the juice from the oranges and put in a pan with the wine. Simmer to reduce by half. Remove from the heat and add the butter and cream stirring until smooth. Add the orange rind and season to taste. Arrange the drained asparagus on individual plates and spoon the sauce over. Garnish with orange slices and parsley sprigs.

Serves 4–6

BROCCOLI & ALMOND TERRINE

This simple terrine, looks very pretty on a dinner party table. Serve with quick tomato sauce (see p. 77).

Oil 2 tbsp (30 ml)
Medium-sized onion, finely chopped 1
Garlic clove, crushed 1
Brown rice 4 oz (100 g)
Vegetable stock ½ pt (300 ml) (see p. 10)
Dried tarragon 1 tsp (5 ml)
Agar flakes 1 tbsp (15 ml) (see p. 5)
Broccoli 1 lb (450 g)
Cauliflower florets 8 oz (225 g)
Flaked almonds, toasted 4 oz (100 g)
Soya sauce 1 tbsp (15 ml)
Salt & pepper to taste

Heat the oil in a saucepan and add the onion and garlic. Sauté gently until transparent. Add the rice, stock, tarragon and agar flakes. Cut the stalks from the broccoli and dice neatly. Add to the saucepan, cover and cook gently until the rice is very soft and all the water is absorbed, approximately 45 minutes. Meanwhile, steam the cauliflower and broccoli florets lightly until just tender. Set aside. When the rice mixture is cooked, combine all ingredients together. Press firmly into a 2 lb (900 g) loaf tin or terrine dish that has been lined with a piece of cling film. Chill thoroughly. To serve, turn on to serving dish. Remove cling film, slice and serve.

Serves 6–8

BRIOCHE DOUGH

This enriched yeast dough can be used for brioche rolls
or as a crust for en croute dishes
(see Mushroom Brioche p. 52).

Milk 2 tbsp (30 ml)
Fresh yeast ½ oz (15 g)
Wholemeal flour 8 oz (225 g)
Salt ½ tsp (2.5 ml)
Unrefined brown sugar ½ oz (15 g)
Free-range eggs 2
Butter at room temperature 3 oz (75 g)
Beaten egg to glaze

Gently heat the milk until tepid then blend with the
yeast in a small bowl. Place the flour, salt and sugar in a
mixing bowl. Mix in the yeast and eggs, one at a time.
Knead for 10 minutes either using a mixer or by hand
on a floured board. Next work in the butter a little at a
time until it is completely incorporated. The dough
should be smooth, glossy and quite soft. Place in a
floured bowl, cover and leave in a warm place for about
1 hour or until the dough has doubled in size. Turn on
to a floured board and knock back by gently kneading
for 5 minutes. If time allows, cover the bowl again and
refrigerate overnight. Knead lightly, then shape the
dough into 8 balls. Place on a greased baking sheet
cover with oiled polythene, and leave to rise until
doubled in size. Glaze with beaten egg then bake at
425°F/220°C/gas mark 7 for 15–20 minutes until golden
brown.
***

MUSHROOM BRIOCHE

Brioche dough 1 quantity (see p. 51)
Butter 1 oz (25 g)
Small onion, finely chopped 1
Mushrooms, finely chopped 8 oz (225 g)
Dried thyme ½ tsp (2.5 ml)
Wholemeal flour 2 tbsp (30 ml)
Soured cream 5 tbsp (75 ml)
Salt & pepper to taste
Beaten egg to glaze

Melt the butter and sauté the onion and mushroom until light golden. Stir in the thyme and flour and cook, stirring until the mixture is fairly dry. Leave to go cold. Stir in the soured cream and season to taste.

On a lightly floured surface, divide the dough into 8 pieces. Shape each one into a round and roll out as thinly as possible. Spoon one eighth of the mushroom mixture into the centre of each. Brush edges with beaten egg then fold the dough into the centre to completely encase the filling. Seal well. Invert on to lightly greased baking sheets. Brush with beaten egg and bake at 400°F/200°C/gas mark 6 for about 20 minutes until risen and golden. Serve warm with a salad garnish.

Serves 8
***

SPICY ONION FRITTERS

Serve these tasty fritters with a minty yoghourt sauce.
(See p. 79)

Natural yoghourt ½ pt (300 ml)
Wholemeal flour 6 oz (175 g)
Salt 1 tsp (5 ml)
Lemon 1
Chilli powder ½ tsp (2.5 ml)
Mustard powder 1 tsp (5 ml)
Large onions, cut into wedge-shaped chunks 2
Oil for deep frying
Lemon and fresh coriander leaves to garnish

Combine the yoghourt, flour, salt, grated lemon rind
and juice, chilli and mustard powder, in a food
processor or by whisking. The batter should be very
smooth. Stir in the chunks of onion. Heat the oil and
test the temperature by dropping in a little batter (it
should first sink, then rise to the surface immediately.
Form the fritters by sliding spoonfuls of onion batter
mixture into the hot oil. Fry on all sides until golden
then lift out with a slotted spoon and drain on
absorbent paper. Serve at once, garnished with lemon
and coriander.

Serves 6

JELLIED VEGETABLE TERRINE

Agar flakes 3 tbsp (45 ml) (see p. 5)
Water ½ pt (300 ml)
Tomato juice ½ pt (300 ml)
Soya sauce 1 tbsp (15 ml)
Parsley, freshly chopped 1 tbsp (15 ml)
Basil, freshly chopped 1 tbsp (15 ml)
Oil 1 tbsp (15 ml)
Medium-sized onion, chopped 1
Garlic clove, crushed 1
Medium-sized carrot, chopped 1
Celery stick, sliced 1
Swede, diced 4 oz (100 g)
Small courgette, diced 1
Broccoli florets 2 oz (50 g)
Leek, sliced 1
Mushrooms, sliced 4 oz (100 g)
Salt & pepper to taste
Large spinach leaves 6–8

Boil the agar flakes in the water until dissolved. Remove from the heat and add the tomato juice, soya sauce and fresh herbs. Heat the oil in a large saucepan. Add the onion, garlic, carrot, celery and swede. Cover and cook gently for 15 minutes without browning.

Add the courgette, broccoli, leeks and mushrooms and continue cooking until just tender, ensuring the vegetables remain their bright colour. Season to taste. Blanch the spinach leaves in boiling water for 1 minute so they just wilt. Drain. Rinse a 2 pt (1.2 l) terrine dish, glass bowl or mould with cold water. Line with the spinach leaves allowing them to come over the top of the terrine. Pack with the cooked mixed vegetables and pour over the tomato agar liquid. (If this has begun to set, re-heat to the liquid state again). Fold down the spinach leaves to completely cover the filling. Chill and allow to set before turning on to a serving plate and slicing.

Serves 8

MUSHROOM BEIGNETS

Serve these with yoghourt sauce (see p. 79),
flavoured with dill.

CHOUX PASTRY
Butter 2 oz (50 g)
Water ¼ pt (150 ml)
Wholemeal flour 2½ oz (65 g)
Salt a pinch
Free-range eggs, beaten 2
Strong flavoured hard cheese, grated 2 oz (50 g)
French mustard 1 tbsp (15 ml)
Paprika ½ tsp (2.5 ml)
Medium-sized button mushrooms 24
Oil for deep frying

Place the butter and water in a saucepan over medium
heat until the butter melts. Bring to the boil, then
immediately add the flour and salt and cook, beating
well with a wooden spoon until the mixture leaves the
sides of the pan and forms a 'ball'. Leave to cool slightly
then beat in the egg a little at a time, then add the
cheese, mustard and paprika. Wipe the mushrooms
and stir into the cheese mixture to evenly coat them.
Heat the oil to 350–375°F/180–190°C (the oil is ready
when a test-piece of mixture bubbles and rises to the
surface) and carefully drop each mushroom coated by
cheese mixture into the pan. Cook in batches of 6 for
4–5 minutes each until crisp and golden. Drain on
absorbent kitchen paper. Keep warm whilst you fry
remaining batches. Serve at once.

Serves 4–6

CHEESE NUGGETS WITH TOMATO & BASIL SAUCE

CHOUX PASTRY
Butter 2 oz (50 g)
Water ¼ pt (150 ml)
Wholemeal flour 2½ oz (65 g)
Salt a pinch
Free-range eggs, beaten 2
Cheddar cheese, grated 2 oz (50 g)
Prepared mustard 1 tbsp (15 ml)
Paprika ½ tsp (2.5 ml)

Tomato & basil sauce 1 quantity (see p. 78)
Cherry tomatoes and fresh basil leaves to garnish

Place the butter and water in a saucepan over medium heat until the butter melts. Bring to the boil and immediately add all the flour and salt, beating well until the mixture leaves the sides of the pan and forms a 'ball'. Leave to cool slightly then beat in the egg a little at a time then add the cheese, mustard and paprika.

Either spoon or pipe 24 small mounds on to greased baking sheets and bake at 400°F/200°C/gas mark 6 for 25–30 minutes until crisp and golden.

Serve the cheese nuggets with the sauce and garnish with cherry tomatoes and fresh basil leaves.

Serves 4–6

EXOTIC SALAD STARTER

Spinach leaves, finely shredded 2 oz (50 g)
Iceberg lettuce, finely shredded 4 oz (100 g)
French dressing 3 tbsp (45 ml) (see p. 76)
Papaya 1
Avocado 1
Cashew nuts, toasted 1 oz (25 g)

Toss the salad leaves in half the dressing and arrange
on individual plates. Peel, remove seeds and slice the
papaya. Peel, remove stone and slice the avocado. Mix
with the cashew nuts and remaining dressing and
arrange on top of the leaves. Alternatively toss all
ingredients together and serve at once.

Serves 4–6

STOP-GO SALAD

A gaily coloured starter of reds and greens with a
delicious mixture of flavours – choose it for a summer
supper party.

Radish 2 oz (50 g)
Cucumber 6 oz (175 g)
Strawberries 6 oz (175 g)
Kiwi fruit 2
Fresh mint, chopped 1 tbsp (15 ml)
French dressing 4 tbsp (60 ml) (see p. 76)
Mint sprigs and whole strawberries to garnish

Thinly slice the radish and cucumber. Slice the
strawberries and kiwi fruit. Arrange on 4 individual
plates or one large plate. Mix the mint with the French
dressing and pour over just before serving. Garnish
with mint sprigs and whole strawberries.

Serves 4

ALSACE ONION TARTLETS

This delicious recipe was brought back from a summer holiday in Alsace. Serve them hot from the oven with a glass of chilled white wine.

Wholemeal pastry
made with 100% wholemeal flour 4 oz (100 g)

FILLING
Butter or margarine 1 oz (25 g)
100% wholemeal flour 1 oz (25 g)
Milk 2 tbsp (30 ml)
Onions, grated 8 oz (225 g)
Free-range egg, beaten 1
Salt & pepper to taste
French mustard 1 tsp (5 ml)
Nutter ½ oz (15 g) (see p. 6)

Roll out the pastry on a lightly floured board. Cut 12 circles using a 2½ in (7 cm) pastry cutter and line a tray of patty tins. Melt the butter in a saucepan. Add the flour and cook stirring for 1 minute. Remove from the heat and gradually blend in the milk. Cook for 2 minutes then allow to cool slightly. Stir the onions into the thick paste then add the egg, seasoning and mustard. Spoon this mixture into the pastry cases and top each with a scraping of Nutter. Bake at 400°F/200°C/gas mark 6 for 20–25 minutes until golden brown.

Serves 6
***

BAKED SAMOSAS

FILLING
Oil 2 tsp (10 ml)
Small onion, finely chopped 1
Garlic clove, crushed 1
Root ginger, roughly chopped ½ in (1.5 cm)
Cumin seeds ½ tsp (2.5 ml)
Ground coriander ¼ tsp (1.25 ml)
Garam masala ¼ tsp (1.25 ml)
Chilli powder a pinch
Small potato, diced 1
Green split peas, soaked overnight 2 oz (50 g)
Water 7 fl oz (200 ml)
Stock cube ½
Parsley, chopped 2 tbsp (30 ml)
Spring onions, chopped 2
Lemon juice 1 tsp (5 ml)
Salt & pepper to taste
Wholemeal pastry made with wholemeal flour 4 oz (100 g)
replacing the baking powder with mustard powder and adding
1 tsp (5 ml) cumin seeds
Egg, beaten to glaze

Heat the oil and sauté the onion and garlic until
transparent. Place the ginger in a garlic press and
squeeze out the juice, add this with the spices, potato,
drained split peas, water and stock cube. Cover and
simmer gently for about 45 minutes until soft and the
water is absorbed. Cool, stir in the parsley, spring
onions, lemon juice and season to taste. Divide the
pastry into 6 pieces and roll into neat thin rounds. Cut
each in half to give 12 semi-circles. Divide the pea
mixture between the pastry shapes. Brush the edges
with beaten egg and fold into a cone shape sealing the
edges well. Repeat with remaining ones. Place on a
baking sheet, brush with beaten egg and bake at 400°F/
200°C/gas mark 6 for 15–20 minutes until golden. Serve
with a salad garnish.

Serves 6
***

CHEESY VEGETABLE TERRINE

Courgettes, sliced in half lengthways 2
Carrot, cut in long thin strips 1
Broccoli florets 4 oz (100 g)
Red pepper, deseeded and sliced lengthways 1
French beans, topped and tailed 3 oz (75 g)
Spinach leaves 6 oz (175 g)
Mushroom caps 3 oz (75 g)
Medium-sized potato, diced 1
Onion, finely chopped 1
Garlic clove, crushed 1
Low-fat soft cheese 4 oz (100 g)
Cheddar cheese, grated 3 oz (75 g)
Free-range eggs 3
Milk 2 fl oz (50 ml)
Salt & pepper to taste
Butter or margarine ½ oz (15 g)

Prepare the vegetables. In turn, blanch the courgettes, carrot, broccoli, red pepper, beans, spinach and mushrooms for 1 minute. Plunge them immediately into cold water then drain. Boil the potatoes until tender, about 10 minutes. Mix the onion, garlic, cheeses, eggs, milk and seasoning. Stir in the cooled cooked potato.

Line an oiled 2 pt (1.2 l) terrine dish or 2 lb (900 g) loaf tin with some of the spinach leaves. Layer the vegetables in the terrine, starting with the courgettes and alternating with a little cheese mixture. When all the vegetables are used up (or when there is no more room) finish with the cheese mixture and cover with a layer of spinach leaves. Dot with butter or margarine, cover and bake standing in a roasting tin of water, at 400°F/200°C/gas mark 6 for 30–40 minutes, or until set. Allow to cool before turning out and slicing.

Serves 8

RAINBOW TERRINE

Carrots 12 oz (350 g)
Parsnips 12 oz (350 g)
Broccoli 12 oz (350 g)
Free-range eggs 3
Double cream 2 tbsp (30 ml)
Lemon rind, finely grated 1 tsp (5 ml)
Ground nutmeg, a pinch
Spring onion, chopped 1 oz (25 g)
Salt & pepper to taste
Carrot curls and tops to garnish

Roughly chop each of the vegetables, then steam separately until tender, 15–20 minutes. Purée the carrot with one egg, 1 tbsp (15 ml) cream, lemon rind and season to taste. Purée the parsnips with one egg, remaining cream, nutmeg and season to taste. Purée the broccoli with the spring onion, egg and seasoning. Grease and line a 2 lb (900 g) loaf tin. Spread a layer of one purée on the base of the tin. Spread next one on top carefully, then top with final layer, spreading evenly. Cover. Place the loaf tin in a roasting tin half filled with boiling water, bake at 400°F/200°C/gas mark 6 for about 45 minutes until firm to the touch. Allow to cool before turning out. Garnish with carrot curls and tops. Cut into slices and serve warm or cold with green peppercorn sauce. (see p. 79)

Serves 8

SOUFFLÉD TOMATO SHELLS

Large Mediterranean tomatoes
weighing about 8 oz (225 g) each 4
Butter 1 oz (25 g)
Wholemeal flour 2 tbsp (30 ml)
Mustard powder a pinch
Double cream 4 tbsp (60 ml)
Free-range eggs, separated 2
Cheddar or Gruyère or
Parmesan cheese, grated 3 oz (75 g)
(or a mixture of all three)
Salt & pepper to taste

Remove the lids from the tomatoes and carefully
remove the centre and seeds, leaving the shells intact.
Stand them upside down on kitchen paper to drain
well. Melt the butter and stir in the flour, mustard
powder, cream, egg yolks and cheese. Season
generously. Whisk the egg whites until stiff and fold in
to the mixture. Place the tomatoes in individual
ovenproof dishes and fill with the cheese mixture. Bake
at 350°F/180°C/gas mark 4 for 30–35 minutes until risen
and golden and just firm when lightly shaken.

Serves 4

WATERCRESS, MUSHROOM & WALNUT ROULADE

This unusual roulade is really a soufflé omelette, baked in the oven. Serve hot or cold.

FILLING
Oil 1 tbsp (15 ml)
Mushrooms, chopped 4 oz (100 g)
Wholemeal flour 2 tbsp (30 ml)
Milk ¼ pt (150 ml)
French mustard 1 tsp (5 ml)
Soya sauce 1 tsp (5 ml)
Spring onions, finely chopped 2
Walnuts, finely chopped 1 oz (25 g)
Mayonnaise 4 tbsp (60 ml) (see p. 76)
Salt & pepper to taste

ROULADE
Watercress, trimmed 1 bunch
Lemon juice 1 tsp (5 ml)
Free-range eggs, separated 4
Watercress sprigs to garnish
Soured cream to serve

Heat the oil and sauté the mushrooms. Stir in the flour and cook, stirring for 1–2 minutes. Stir in the milk and cook, stirring until thickened. Add French mustard, soya sauce, spring onion and walnuts. Cool. Add the mayonnaise and season to taste. Grease and line with non-stick paper a swiss roll tin 13 × 9 in (33 × 23 cm). Chop the watercress in a food processor with the lemon juice and egg yolks. Whisk the egg whites with a pinch of salt until stiff. Fold in the watercress mixture and transfer to the lined tin. Level the surface and bake at 400°F/200°C/gas mark 6 for 10 minutes until risen and firm to the touch. Carefully turn out on to a sheet of greaseproof paper. Spread with the filling and roll up from a short end. Serve in slices. Garnish with watercress and serve with soured cream.

Serves 8

SPICY LENTIL, SPINACH & TOFU TARTLETS

Wholemeal pastry made with
wholemeal flour 5 oz (150 g)
Oil 1 tbsp (15 ml)
Medium-sized onion, diced 1
Garlic clove, crushed 2
Turmeric 1 tsp 5 ml
Paprika 1 tsp (5 ml)
Ground coriander 1 tsp (5 ml)
Ground cumin 1 tsp (5 ml)
Red lentils 4 oz (100 g)
Water 1 pt (600 ml)
Tomato purée 2 tsp (10 ml)
Fresh basil, chopped 1 tbsp (15 ml)
Salt & pepper to taste
Spinach 6 oz (175 g)
Tofu 8 oz (225 g) (see p. 7)
Lemon, juice of ½
Agar flakes 1 tbsp (15 ml) (see p. 5)
Soya sauce 2 tsp (10 ml)

Roll out the pastry and stamp out twelve 2½ inch (7 cm) rounds. Use to line a tray of patty tins. Heat the oil and sauté the onion, garlic and spices for 5 minutes. Add the lentils and ¾ pt (450 ml) water and simmer gently for 15–20minutes until the water is absorbed. Cool, then add the tomato purée, basil and seasoning.

Cook the spinach in boiling, salted water until just wilted – about 2 minutes. Drain, cool and squeeze out excess liquid. Purée with the tofu and lemon juice in a liquidizer or food processor. Place a spoonful of spicy lentils in each pastry case. Cover with the spinach mixture and bake at 400°F/200°C gas mark 6 for 20–25 minutes. Boil the agar flakes in the remaining water and soya sauce until dissolved. Cool slightly then spoon over each tartlet. Leave to set.

Makes 12

SESAME SHROUDED LEEKS

CHEESE PASTRY
Wholemeal flour 3 oz (75 g)
Curd or cream cheese 4 oz (100 g)
Butter, softened 2 oz (50 g)
Salt, a pinch
Medium leeks 4
Vegetable stock 1 pt (600 ml) (see p. 10)
Egg white to glaze
Sesame seeds 2 tbsp (30 ml)
Cherry tomatoes and fresh basil to garnish

Work all the ingredients for the pastry together until evenly mixed, to give a soft dough. Chill until required. Trim the leeks to an even length, then place whole in the stock in a wide, shallow pan. Bring to the boil, reduce heat, cover and simmer for about 5 minutes until just tender. Leave to go cold in the stock. Drain and squeeze out in a clean tea towel to remove excess moisture. Cut in half crossways. Roll out the pastry thinly on a lightly floured board and cut into 8 strips the width of the leeks and long enough to completely encase them. Wrap the leeks in the pastry, sealing the edges well. Brush with beaten egg white and coat in sesame seeds. Bake at 400°F/200°C/gas mark 6 for about 20 minutes until crisp and golden. Garnish with cherry tomatoes and basil leaves and serve warm with quick tomato sauce (see p. 77).

Serves 4

MILLET & TOFU CROQUETTES

These croquettes are particularly good made with
oak-smoked tofu.

Whole millet 5 oz (150 g)
Vegetable stock ¾ pt (450 ml) (see p. 10)
Tofu 12 oz (350 g) (see p. 7)
Soya sauce 1 tbsp (15 ml)
Lemon juice 1 tbsp (15 ml)
Peanuts, finely chopped 2 oz (50 g)
Brazil nuts, finely chopped 1 oz (25 g)
Parsley, chopped 2 tbsp (30 ml)
Salt & pepper to taste

COATING
Soya flour 1 oz (25 g)
Water 4 fl oz (100 ml)
Millet flakes 2 oz (50 g)
Oil for deep frying

Dry roast the millet in a heavy-based pan until it begins
to turn light brown. Add the stock, cover and cook for
30–40 minutes until the millet is soft and the liquid is
absorbed. Cool. Place all the ingredients into a food
processor and blend until smooth. Season to taste.
Chill. Shape into 16 croquettes. Mix together the soya
flour and water. Dip the croquettes in the batter and
then roll in millet flakes to evenly coat. Heat the oil to
350–375°F/180–190°C and fry the croquettes until crisp
and golden, 4–5 minutes. Drain on absorbent paper.
Serve at once with a salad garnish.

Serves 8 (makes 16)
***

SPICY LENTIL PATTIES

Red lentils 8 oz (225 g)
Water ¾ pt (450 ml)
Vegetable extract 1 tsp (5 ml)
Oil 1 tbsp (15 ml)
Onion, chopped 4 oz (100g)
Green pepper, chopped 3 oz (75 g)
Ground cumin ½ tsp (2.5 ml)
Paprika ¼ tsp (1.25 ml)
Curry powder ½ tsp (2.5 ml)
Chilli powder a pinch
Coriander, freshly chopped 1 tbsp (15 ml)
Lemon juice 1 tbsp (15 ml)
Parsley, freshly chopped 1 tbsp (15 ml)
Salt & pepper to taste

COATING
Soya flour 1 oz (25 g)
Water 4 fl oz (100 ml)
Fine oatmeal 1½ oz (40 g)
Toasted wholemeal breadcrumbs, finely ground 1½ oz (40 g)
Oil for deep frying

Cook the lentils in the measured water and vegetable extract over gentle heat until the lentils are tender and all the liquid has been absorbed – about 20 minutes. Heat the oil and sauté the onion until transparent. Add the peppers and continue cooking until very soft. Add the dry spices and cook for a further 3–4 minutes. Combine all the ingredients and chill. Shape the lentil mixture into 12 small patties. Mix the soya flour and water together to give a pouring batter. Combine the oatmeal and breadcrumbs. Dip the patties in the batter and then in the oatmeal mixture to evenly coat. Reshape as required. Heat the oil to 350–375°F/180–190°C and deep fry the patties in batches until crisp and golden – about 3–4 minutes. Drain on absorbent paper. Serve at once with natural yoghourt and salad garnish.

Serves 6 (makes 12)
***

CARROT-STUFFED AVOCADO

Carrots, cooked and roughly mashed 6 oz (175 g)
Curd cheese 4 oz (100 g)
Walnuts, chopped 1 oz (25 g)
Spring onions, finely chopped 2
Salt & pepper to taste
Ripe avocados 2
Lemon juice, a sprinkling
Curly endive, spring onion and walnut halves to garnish

Combine the first 4 ingredients and season generously.
Halve the avocados, remove the stones and sprinkle
with lemon juice. Fill the cavity in each pear with the
carrot mixture and bake at 350°F/180°C/gas mark 4 for 20
minutes until heated through. Serve at once garnished
with curly endive, spring onions and walnut halves.

Serves 4

MARINATED VEGETABLES

Olive oil 4 fl oz (100 ml)
Small lemon, juice of 1
Chopped parsley 2 tbsp (30 ml)
Garlic cloves, crushed 1–2
Salt & pepper to taste
Button mushrooms 8 oz (225 g)
Thin green beans 4 oz (100 g)
Medium leeks, cut into 1 in (2.5 cm) lengths 2
Red pepper, deseeded and diced 1

Combine the first 4 ingredients. Wipe the mushrooms,
and add to the marinade. Place each type of vegetable
in boiling water and bring back to a rapid boil. Drain
and add to the mushrooms. Leave to marinate for
several hours. Toss well and season to taste.

Serves 4

LENTIL & MUSHROOM PATTIES

Oil 1 tbsp (15 ml)
Mushrooms, chopped 4 oz (100 g)
Green lentils 4 oz (100 g)
Vegetable stock ½ pt (300 ml)
Vegetable extract 1 tsp (5 ml)
Bayleaf 1
Dried rosemary ½ tsp (2.5 ml)
Dried thyme ½ tsp (2.5 ml)
Onions, chopped 3 oz (75 g)
Tomato purée 1 tbsp (15 ml)
Fresh basil, chopped 1 tbsp (15 ml)
Fresh parsley, chopped 2 tbsp (30 ml)
Salt & pepper to taste

COATING
Soya flour 1 oz (25 g)
Water 4 fl oz (100 ml)
Fine oatmeal 1 oz (25 g)
Toasted wholemeal breadcrumbs 1 oz (25 g)
Oil for deep frying

Heat half the oil and sauté the mushrooms, drain well, reserving any cooking liquid. Cook the lentils with the vegetable stock, reserved mushroom liquid, vegetable extract and herbs over medium heat, until the lentils are soft and all the liquid has been absorbed – up to 45 minutes. Add extra liquid if necessary. Sauté the onions in the remaining oil until transparent. Mix together the mushrooms, lentils, and onions, then add the remaining ingredients. Season to taste. Chill. Shape into 12 small cakes. Mix together the soya flour and water. Mix together the oatmeal and toasted breadcrumbs. Dip the cakes first in the soya batter and then in the breadcrumbs mixture until evenly coated. Reshape as necessary. Heat the oil to 350–375°F/180–190°C and fry the patties in 2 batches – about 3 minutes each until golden brown. Drain on absorbent paper. Serve at once with a salad garnish.

SPLIT PEA, RICE &
LEMON PATTIES

Green split peas 4 oz (100 g)
Bayleaf 1
Water ¾–1 pt (450–600 ml)
Vegetable extract 1 tsp (5 ml)
Brown rice 2 oz (50 g)
Oil 1 tbsp (15 ml)
Onion, finely chopped 4 oz (100 g)
Lemon rind 1 tsp (5 ml)
Lemon juice 1 tbsp (15 ml)
Soya sauce 2 tsp (10 ml)
Chopped parsley 2 tbsp (30 ml)
Salt & pepper to taste

COATING
Soya flour 1 oz (25 g)
Water 4 fl oz (100 ml)
Fine oatmeal 1½ oz (40 g)
Toasted wholemeal breadcrumbs 1½ oz (40 g)
Oil for deep frying

Place split peas, bayleaf, ½ pt (300 ml) water and vegetable extract in a saucepan. Bring to the boil, reduce heat, cover and simmer for about 20 minutes, stirring occasionally. Add the rice and remaining ¼ pt (150 ml) water. Cover and simmer for 20–25 minutes, adding extra water if necessary and stirring from time to time. Cook until pulpy and no free liquid remains. Cool. Heat the oil and sauté the onion until transparent. Mix all the ingredients together and season to taste. Chill. Shape into 8 patties. Mix the soya flour with the water. Mix the oatmeal with the toasted breadcrumbs. Dip the patties first in soya batter and then in oatmeal mixture until evenly coated. Reshape as necessary. Heat the oil to 350–375°F/180–190°C and fry the patties for 3–4 minutes until crisp and golden. Drain on absorbent paper. Serve at once with a salad garnish.

Serves 4 (makes 8)
***

CHEESE & ONION POUCHES

FILLING
Onion, finely chopped 8 oz (225 g)
Yeast extract 1 tsp (5 ml)
Water 5 tbsp (75 ml)
Cream cheese 3 oz (75 g)
Cheddar cheese, grated 3 oz (75 g)
Salt & pepper to taste

PASTRY
Wholemeal flour 8 oz (225 g)
Fresh basil, chopped 1 tbsp (15 ml)
or dried basil 1 tsp (5 ml)
Butter 4 oz (100 g)
Iced water 3 tbsp (45 ml)
Egg, beaten to glaze

Place the onions in a saucepan with the yeast extract and water. Simmer until soft and no free liquid remains. Cool slightly then mix in the cheeses and season to taste. Mix the flour and basil together, then rub in the butter until the mixture resembles fine crumbs. Add sufficient water to mix to a firm dough. On a lightly floured surface roll out the pastry to a rectangle about 10 × 16 in (25 × 40 cm) and cut into 8 small rectangles. Divide the filling between the pastry, wet the edges, then fold the pastry over to completely encase the filling. Seal the edges well and transfer to a baking tray. Mark the tops with a fork and brush with beaten egg to glaze. Bake at 400°F/200°C/gas mark 6 for about 20 minutes until golden. Serve warm with salad.

Makes 8
***

LEMON & AVOCADO SORBET

Large lemons 3
Water 8 fl oz (250 ml)
Agar flakes 1 tbsp (15 ml) (see p. 5)
Pale unrefined brown sugar 3 oz (75 g)
Large ripe avocado 1

Finely grate the rind from 1 lemon, then squeeze the juice from all 3 lemons. Place the water in a saucepan and add the agar flakes. Bring to a simmer and simmer gently for 2–3 minutes until dissolved. Add the sugar, and stir over gentle heat until the sugar has dissolved.

Stir in the lemon rind and juice and transfer to a rigid container. Freeze until 'slushy'.

Peel, remove stone and mash the avocado. Beat into the sorbet until evenly mixed, then freeze until required.

Serves 4–6
***

ICED TOMATO CRUSH

Ripe tomatoes, skinned and deseeded 1 lb (450 g)
Tomato purée 2 tbsp (30 ml)
Green pepper deseeded and finely chopped ½
Celery stick, finely chopped 1
Spring onion chopped 1 tbsp (15 ml)
or
Clove garlic, crushed 1
Lemon, juice of ½
Chilli powder a pinch
Salt & pepper to taste
Celery leaves to garnish

Purée the tomatoes in a liquidizer. Stir in all the
remaining ingredients and season to taste. Transfer to a
rigid container and freeze until slushy. Beat well and
freeze to a soft frozen texture. Serve garnished with
celery leaves.

Serves 4–6
***

GINGERED FRUIT STARTER

Large grapefruit, (preferably Ruby) 1
Large oranges 2
Melon ¼
Unrefined sugar crystallized ginger 1 oz (25 g)
French dressing 2 tbsp (30 ml) (see p. 76)
Belgian endive leaves
or watercress sprigs to garnish

Using a small serrated knife, peel the grapefruit and
oranges removing all the white pith. Cut into slices, or
remove segments from all the fruit. Dice the melon, and
chop the ginger. Mix the fruits together with the ginger
and French dressing. Spoon onto individual plates and
garnish with Belgian endive or watercress.

Serves 4

GARLIC BUTTERED BREAD

Butter, at room temperature 4 oz (100 g)
Garlic cloves, crushed 1–2
Fresh parsley, chopped 2 tbsp (30 ml)
Freshly baked wholemeal
bread in stick shape 1 loaf

Place the butter in a bowl. Beat in the crushed garlic and the chopped parsley. Cut the bread stick in ½ in (1.5 cm) slices taking care not to cut quite all the way through. Butter between the slices then wrap the loaf in foil. Place in the oven at 400°F/200°C/gas mark 6 for 10–15 minutes or until the bread is hot and the butter melted into it.

MELBA TOAST

An attractive way of serving light crispy toast with all sorts of dips and starters.

One-day-old 100% wholemeal bread, thinly sliced.

Cut the bread into wafer-thin slices with a sharp, serrated knife. Arrange in a single layer on a baking sheet and bake in the oven at 400°F/200°C/gas mark 6 for 7–8 minutes until really crisp and golden. Cool on a wire tray. Keep in an airtight container.

WHOLEMEAL CROUTONS

One-day-old 100% wholemeal bread
Oil for frying

Cut the bread into ¼–½ in (1–1.5 cm) cubes and fry in hot oil until crisp and golden on all sides. Drain on absorbent paper.

Variation
Add sliced cloves of garlic to the oil to give the croutons a garlic flavour.

CRANKS FRENCH DRESSING

Lemons, juice of 2
Cider or wine vinegar 4 tbsp (60 ml)
Salt 1½ tsp (7.5 ml)
Pepper ½ tsp (2.5 ml)
French mustard 1 tbsp (15 ml)
Unrefined brown sugar 2 tsp (10 ml)
Oil ¾ pt (450 ml)

Put the lemon juice, vinegar, salt, pepper, mustard and sugar into a jug. Whisk with a fork until evenly blended, then slowly work in the oil.

or put all the ingredients together in a liquidizer and blend for a few seconds.

or shake all the ingredients together in a screw-topped jar.

Makes about 1 pt (600 ml)

CRANKS MAYONNAISE

Free-range egg 1
Salt ½ tsp (2.5 ml)
French mustard ½ tsp (2.5 ml)
Cider or wine vinegar 2 tsp (10 ml)
Oil ½ pt (300 ml)

Break the egg into a liquidizer. Add the salt, mustard and vinegar. Blend for 10 seconds. While the liquidizer is switched on, slowly feed in the oil through the lid. As the oil is added the mayonnaise will become thick. To make the mayonnaise by hand, beat the egg, salt, mustard and vinegar together in a basin using a wooden spoon or balloon whisk. Then add the oil, drop by drop, until half has been used. Continue adding in very small quantities until it has all been incorporated.

Makes ½ pt (300 ml)

QUICK TOMATO SAUCE

This basic recipe produces a good chunky sauce. It can also be blended for a smoother texture, enriched, spiced or flavoured with wine. Serve with terrines and en croute dishes.

Oil 1 tbsp (15 ml)
Onion, finely chopped 1
Garlic clove, crushed 1
Tomatoes, roughly chopped 12 oz (350 g)
Tomato purée 2 tsp (10 ml)
Tomato juice ¼ pt (150 ml)
Bayleaf 1
Apple concentrate or honey 1 tsp (5 ml) (see p. 5)
Salt & pepper to taste
Soya sauce 2 tsp (10 ml)
Sherry, dry or medium 1 tbsp (15 ml)
Fresh basil 1 tbsp (15 ml)

Heat the oil and sauté the onion and garlic until transparent. Add the tomatoes, tomato purée and juice, bayleaf and apple concentrate. Cook for 5–10 minutes uncovered and on a medium heat to allow the liquid to reduce. Add the remaining ingredients and remove the bayleaf.

Variations
1 Blend until smooth in a liquidizer or food processor.
2 Add 1–2 tbsp (15–30 ml) cream or yoghourt.
3 Substitute ¼ pt (150 ml) of red wine for the tomato juice – omit sherry.
4 Add pinch of chilli powder, and cumin seeds to taste.

Serves 4–6
***

TARRAGON CREAM SAUCE

Butter or margarine 1 oz 25 g
Small onion, very finely chopped 1
Dried tarragon 1 tsp (5 ml)
Whipping cream ¼ pt (150 ml)
Sherry, medium or dry 2 tbsp (30 ml)
Salt & pepper to taste

Melt the butter in a small saucepan. Sauté the onion and tarragon gently for 5 minutes. Add the cream and sherry and simmer to reduce to a coating consistency. Season to taste.

Serves 4–6

TOMATO & BASIL SAUCE

Butter 1 oz (25 g)
Small onion, finely diced 1
Tomatoes, roughly chopped 8 oz (225 g)
Wholemeal flour 2 tbsp (30 ml)
Milk ¼ pt (150 ml)
Vegetable stock ¼ pt (150 ml) (see p. 10)
Basil, freshly chopped 1 tbsp (15ml)
Salt & pepper to taste

Melt the butter and sauté the onion until transparent. Add the tomato and cook until softened. Stir in the flour and cook for 1–2 minutes. Stir in the milk and stock and simmer gently for 5 minutes until thickened. Add the basil and purée until fairly smooth. Season to taste.

Serves 4–6

YOGHOURT SAUCE

The fresh clean flavour of this sauce goes particularly
well with fritters, patties and rissoles.

Natural yoghourt ½ pt (300 ml)
Small onion, finely chopped 1
Lemon, juice of 1
Apple concentrate or honey 1 tsp (5 ml) (see p. 5)
Salt & pepper to taste

Combine all ingredients, mixing until smooth. If
wished, add chopped fresh herbs such as parsley, dill,
fennel, chervil or mint to taste.

Serves 4–6

GREEN PEPPERCORN SAUCE

Double cream ½ pt (300 ml)
Green peppercorns, crushed 1 tbsp (15 ml)
Lemon juice to taste
Salt to taste

Heat the cream and peppercorns to just below boiling
point. Remove from the heat and leave to infuse for 5
minutes. Add lemon juice and salt to taste.

Serves 8

TOFU & TAHINI DIP

This creamy tasty dip has no added fat and is also suitable for vegans. We recommend a mildly spiced fruit chutney. Serve it with wholemeal toast fingers or carrot and celery sticks.

Tofu, roughly chopped 8 oz (225 g) (see p. 7)
Tahini 2 tsp (10 ml) (see p. 7)
Soya sauce 1 tbsp (15 ml)
Sherry, medium or dry 1 tbsp (15 ml)
Chutney 1–2 tbsp (15–30 ml)
Apple concentrate 1 tbsp (15 ml) (see p. 5)
Salt & pepper to taste
Spring onions, chopped 4
Sesame seeds and spring onions to garnish

Combine all the ingredients except the spring onions in a liquidizer or food processor. Stir in the chopped spring onions and adjust seasoning. Dry roast the sesame seeds until golden in a heavy based pan. Sprinkle over the dip and garnish with extra spring onions.

Serves 4–6

DEVILLED AVOCADO DIP

Large ripe avocado 1
Mayonnaise ¼ pt (150 ml) (see p. 76)
Soured cream ¼ pt (150 ml)
Thick-set natural yoghourt ½ pt (300 ml)
Spring onions, chopped 3
Garlic clove, crushed 1
Olives, green, chopped 1 oz (25 g)
Gherkins, chopped 1 oz (25 g)
Capers, chopped 1 tbsp (15 ml)
Salt & pepper to taste

Peel the avocado, remove the stone then place in a
liquidizer or food processor and work with the
mayonnaise, soured cream and yoghourt until smooth.
Stir in the remaining ingredients and season to taste.
Serve with savoury biscuits or crisp vegetables.

Variation
Spinach avocado dip
Omit yoghourt from basic mixture. Wash 1 lb (450 g)
fresh young spinach leaves, remove coarse stalks, then
cook in a dry pan until wilted and cook rapidly until all
the liquid evaporates. Alternatively squeeze out excess
liquid. Purée spinach with avocado, mayonnaise and
soured cream. Add 8 oz (225 g) cottage cheese with
flavouring ingredients as above.

Serves 8

SPICY AVOCADO &
PINEAPPLE DIP

Based on the Mexican guacamole dip, this refreshing
fruit starter is a favourite in Cranks restaurants. Serve
with Melba toast (see p. 74) or crudités.

Avocado 2
Garlic clove, crushed 1
French dressing 1 tbsp (15 ml) (see p. 76)
Lemon, juice of ½
Chilli powder, a pinch
Salt & pepper to taste
Pineapple, chopped 2 oz (50 g)
Paprika & chopped parsley to garnish

Halve the avocado, remove the stone and scoop out the
flesh. Combine all the ingredients except the pineapple
in a liquidizer or food processor until velvety smooth.
Stir in the chopped pineapple and garnish with a
sprinkling of paprika and a little chopped parsley.

Serves 4

FLAGEOLET BEAN DIP

Flageolet beans, soaked overnight 4 oz (100g)
Ripe avocado, peeled, stoned and mashed 1
Low-fat soft cheese 4 oz (100 g)
Mayonnaise 1 tbsp (15 ml) (see p. 76)
Fresh lime or lemon juice 1 tbsp (15 ml)
Spring onion, chopped 2 tbsp (30 ml)
Large green pepper, deseeded, finely diced ½
Ground cumin ½ tsp (2.5 ml)
Dried oregano ½ tsp (2.5 ml)
Chilli powder a pinch
Salt & pepper to taste

Drain the beans, cover with fresh water. Bring to the
boil and boil for 10 minutes. Reduce heat, cover and
simmer for about 1 hour until tender. Leave to go cold
then drain and mash. Combine all the ingredients
together, beat well and season to taste. Serve with raw
vegetable sticks or bread.

Serves 6

FRUITED CHEESE DIP

Curd or cream cheese 8 oz (225 g)
Natural yoghourt 5 tbsp (60 ml)
Walnuts, chopped 2 oz (50 g)
Fresh dates, chopped 2 oz (50 g)
Spring onion, chopped 2 tbsp (30 ml)
Orange rind, grated 1 tsp (5 ml)

Beat all the ingredients together. Serve with raw
vegetables, crisp biscuits or bread.

Serves 4–6

INDEX

84

Recipes which are suitable for
freezing are marked by asterisks
***